Acknowledgments:

This *Heat Illness Prevention Training Guide* was adapted from materials developed by the Labor Occupational Health Program (LOHP), University of California, Berkeley. These materials are part of the Worker Occupational Safety and Health Training and Education Program (WOSHTEP), which is administered by the Commission on Health and Safety and Workers' Compensation in the Department of Industrial Relations through interagency agreements with LOHP and the Labor Occupational Safety and Health Program (LOSH) at the University of California, Los Angeles (UCLA).

Some of these materials were adapted from *Heat Hazards in Agriculture – a Guide for Employers to Carry Out Tailgate Training for Workers*, developed by The Division of Occupational Safety and Health, better known as Cal/OSHA and Labor Occupational Health Program (LOHP).

For additional information on acknowledgments and technical contributors, please see:
http://www.dir.ca.gov/chswc/reports/CHSWC_HeatAgriculturEnglish.pdf

For More Information:
U.S. Department of Labor
Occupational Safety and Health Administration
1-800-321-OSHA (6742)
TTY 1-877-889-5627
www.osha.gov

> Users are encouraged to photocopy or adapt this information as needed
> for not-for-profit training purposes.
> Please acknowledge CalOSHA and LOHP for producing the materials.

Table of Contents

OSHA Publications
- OSHA Heat Safety Fact Sheet, Publication #3422; English
- OSHA Heat Safety Fact Sheet, Publication #3423; Spanish
- OSHA Worksite Poster, Publication #3431; English
- OSHA Worksite Poster, Publication #3432; Spanish
- OSHA Community Poster, Publication #3435; English
- OSHA Community Poster, Publication #3436; Spanish

For Use in Training
- Rogelio's Story
- Diagram #1. Preventing Heat Illness
- Diagram #2. Health Effects of Heat

The past few summers have shown that the risk of heat illness from high temperatures is one of the most serious challenges to the safety and health of workers.

This training guide will help you plan how to prevent heat illness among your crew and provide training to your workers. The training guide includes the following tools for the supervisor or crew leader to use:

- Complete instructions for teaching workers about heat hazards. *(pages 4-16)*

- Additional resources:
  - A daily checklist to make sure all appropriate precautions are in place each workday. *(page 18)*
  - OSHA Heat Safety Fact Sheet, in English and Spanish, that reviews some of the key information about heat illness. *(pages 19-23)*
  - Easy-to-read OSHA posters, in English and Spanish, for the worksite and the community that you can copy and distribute to workers. *(pages 24-29)*

The training is designed to be:

- **Short** — it's 45 minutes long, but if you'd prefer you can carry it out in three 15-minute sessions as meetings before the work shift or during "shade breaks."

- **Participatory** — for workers to be able to ask questions and have some discussion, which increases the likelihood they will remember the information.

- **Easy to follow** — so a supervisor or crew leader can lead the training.

Why is it important to prevent heat illness?

- Heat illness can be a matter of life and death. Workers die from heat stroke every summer and every death is preventable.

- When heat stroke doesn't kill immediately, it can shut down major body organs causing acute heart, liver, kidney and muscle damage, nervous system problems, and blood disorders.

- Having a serious injury or death occur at work affects everyone at a worksite.

- Workers suffering from heat exhaustion are at greater risk for accidents, since they are less alert and can be confused.

Providing short training sessions can be a very efficient way to reach workers with health and safety information. Like all training, making sure you are effective in communicating the information takes preparation and a real desire to involve your crew in health and safety. In this guide, you will find some advice for trainers that can help encourage discussion and enable workers to be active players in keeping the job safe.

Follow these three steps to prepare for and carry out the training:

1. Read and become familiar with the *Heat Illness Prevention Training Guide* (beginning on page 4).

2. Hold the training.

3. Obtain feedback. To conclude the training, you may want to ask the crew for feedback. Did they understand the material? Was it well presented? Was it helpful and relevant to their particular type of work?

How to use this guide:

The Training Guide is written so that you can easily follow it. It is divided into three 15-minute sessions:

Session 1: Health effects of heat

Session 2: How to respond to symptoms

Session 3: Preventing heat illness

To provide this training, you will be leading a discussion in which you ask questions and encourage participation.

How the guide is formatted:

The training guide will lead you through the training. It includes instructions for you as the trainer as well as questions you can ask to lead a discussion.

- Most of the training guide is made up of the questions and comments that you as the trainer will be reading out loud, or saying once you get to know the material and are comfortable with it. A talking head icon (🗣) is used to show where you will be speaking.

- Instructions to the trainer are numbered and written in ***bold italics***. You do not need to read these out loud.

- The answers to questions are provided in shaded boxes. Wait for the crew to give answers based on what they know, and then add any missing points or clarify any information if needed.

To prepare to teach the training sessions:

1. Spend about 15 minutes becoming familiar with this *Heat Illness Prevention Training Guide*. Read it over and make sure you understand all the information.

2. Fill in the blanks in the Training Guide. Adding these details helps make sure that the safety meeting deals with actual conditions on your own job site.

3. There are three drawings you will use in the sessions. They are on pages 31-33 and you can hold them up to show the crew as you teach. Or you may want to make copies of them ahead of time.

Advice for Trainers

Safety meetings work best if the whole crew actively participates. This makes it more interesting and more likely that people will remember the information you've provided. Here are some ways to encourage everyone to get involved:

- Ask questions instead of simply giving them all the information. After you ask a question, wait a short time to let people think. Then call on volunteers to answer. After workers have provided their answers, use the information in the answer boxes to add any points the crew missed.

- Ask about personal experience. This can help the group see how the topic is relevant to them. You could ask: Has anyone experienced any problems with heat, such as heat cramps? What happened? What did you do to recover?

- Limit the amount of time any one person can talk. If a crew member is talking too much, invite someone else to speak.

- Never make fun of anyone, or put anyone down, especially for asking questions.

- Don't fake it. If you don't know the answer to a question, don't guess or fake the answer. Write the question down and promise to get back to them.

- Stick to the topic. If the crew's questions and comments move too far from the topic, tell them that their concerns can be addressed later, either privately or in another safety meeting.

Training Session #1: Health Effects of Heat
(Time: 15 minutes)

1. Introduce the topic by saying something like this:

Today we are going to talk about how heat can affect you and what symptoms you should watch out for. Heat exhaustion can often affect you before you even realize it, so it's important to be very aware of the signs.

2. Ask the crew these questions:

(Wait for their answers and then use the shaded answer boxes to add any information they missed.)

Just like we can't let a car engine overheat or it shuts down, we don't want your body to get too hot. Let's start by talking about heat — where does the heat come from that causes our bodies to overheat?

> - Hot weather
> - Humid weather
> - Sun – you absorb more heat if you are in the sun
> - Heat our bodies generate when we are physically active and doing hard work

Working outdoors, especially in hot and humid weather, being in the sun, and doing hard physical work is something we have to take seriously.

What are some of the signs you may notice if your body is getting too hot?

> - Headache, dizziness, or fainting
> - Weakness and wet skin
> - Irritability or confusion
> - Thirst, nausea, or vomiting

🗣 These are the early signs that you need to cool off, rest, and drink water to let your body recover. If you don't, you could develop some of the more serious effects of heat.

3. *Show the crew Diagram #1, Preventing Heat Illness, on page 32. Review the following points:*

🗣 Working outdoors is hard work and you will feel sweaty and tired. Workers need to drink water, take shade breaks, and rest to prevent heat problems (point to A in the diagram).

Then, if you feel better, you can go back to work (point to B), but you should still drink water frequently and take another break when you need to. If you don't feel better, talk to your supervisor right away.

4. *Show the crew Diagram #2, Health Effects of Heat, on page 33. Review the following points:*

🗣 This diagram will help us understand what happens when you are affected by heat.

If you are working in the heat, especially if you're not drinking enough water or taking enough breaks, you may get heat exhaustion *(point to C).*

- You may get a headache, experience dizziness, or faint.
- You could get weak or have wet skin
- You may become irritable or confused
- You may be thirsty, nauseous, or vomit. People react differently, so you may have just a few of these symptoms, or most of them.
- If you start to feel confused, or if you vomit or become faint, you may be having a more serious response.

Workers may also develop what is called heat stroke *(point to D).*

- At this point, you may be confused, unable to think clearly, pass out, collapse, or have seizures (fits).

- You may stop sweating. Sweating is the main way our bodies cool off — so not sweating is a very serious emergency.

There have been cases where workers have seemed fine at lunch and a couple of hours later were found having seizures or unconscious. It can happen quickly. The best way to protect ourselves is to prevent heat exhaustion — by drinking plenty of water, taking breaks, and resting to cool off. (Point to A on Diagram #1.)

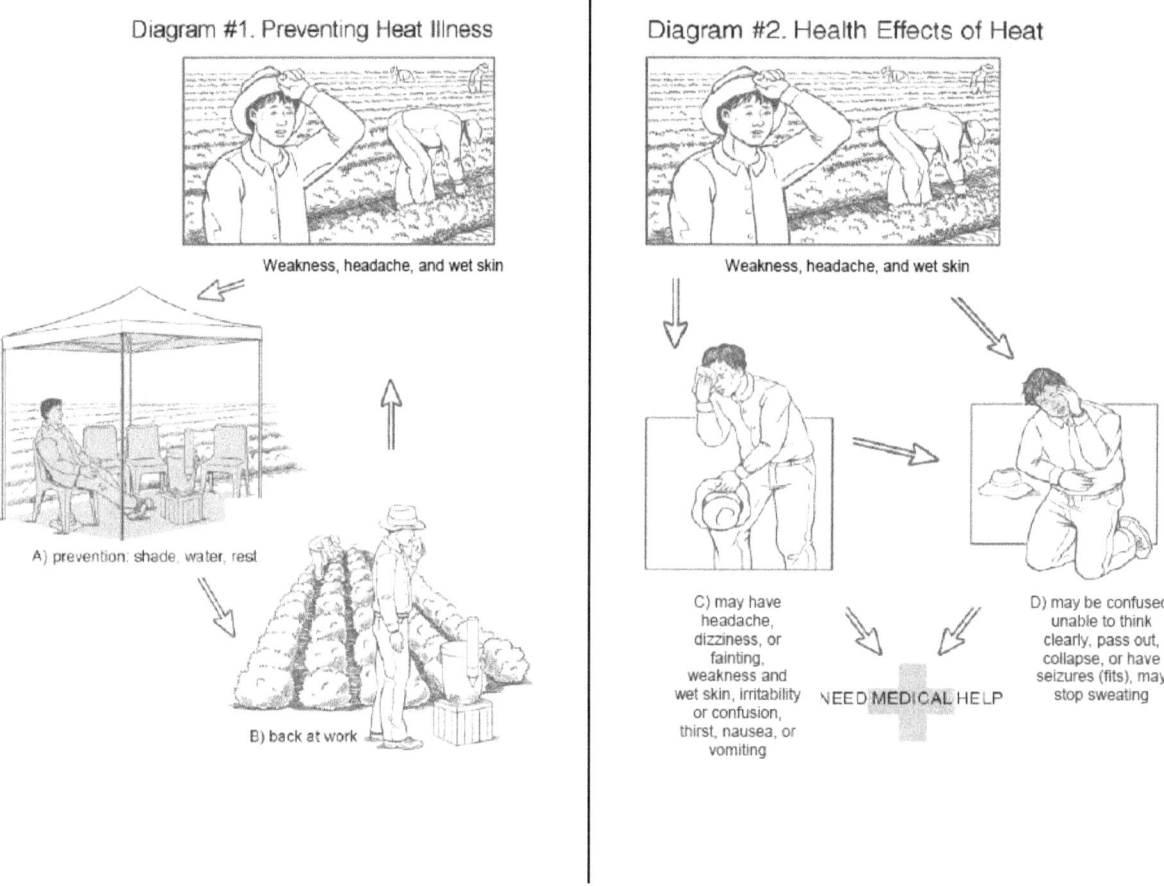

Diagram #1. Preventing Heat Illness

Weakness, headache, and wet skin

A) prevention: shade, water, rest

B) back at work

Diagram #2. Health Effects of Heat

Weakness, headache, and wet skin

C) may have headache, dizziness, or fainting, weakness and wet skin, irritability or confusion, thirst, nausea, or vomiting

NEED MEDICAL HELP

D) may be confused, unable to think clearly, pass out, collapse, or have seizures (fits), may stop sweating

5. Ask the crew these questions:

(Wait for their answers and then use the shaded answer boxes to add any information they missed.)

To review, what are some of the signs that you are developing heat exhaustion?

> - Headache
> - Dizziness or fainting
> - Weakness
> - Wet skin
> - Irritability
> - Thirst
> - Nausea or vomiting
> - WARNING: If you feel FAINT, CONFUSED, or if you VOMIT – you need help FAST!

What are some of the signs of heat stroke?

> - May be confused
> - May be unable to think clearly
> - May pass out
> - May collapse
> - May have seizures (fits)
> - May stop sweating

🗣 Heat illness can affect us all, but some people are at greater risk. What do you think would put a person at greater risk?

> - You aren't used to working in heat or doing heavy work.
>
> - You are new to working outdoors.
>
> - You are not physically fit or are overweight.
>
> - You drink alcohol or take drugs (illegal drugs or prescription medicine).
>
> - You wear heavy, dark, or tight clothing, or use personal protective equipment.
>
> - You had some early heat-related symptoms the day before.

6. Stress the following points:

🗣 Not being used to working in heat is a big problem. Most of the people who died from heat stroke in the past few years were in their first few days on the job or were working during a heat wave. If you haven't worked in hot weather for a week or more, your body needs time to adjust. You need to take more breaks and not do too much strenuous work during your first weeks on the job.

Some health conditions can put you at greater risk of heat illness. These include diabetes, kidney and heart problems, pregnancy, and being overweight. If you have these, it would be good to talk to your doctor about the work you do and ask whether there are any special precautions you need to take.

7. To conclude, ask if anyone has questions, then close by saying:

🗣 Next time, we are going to talk about how you should respond if you or your co-workers are feeling any of these symptoms.

Training Session #2: How to Respond to Symptoms

(Time: 15 minutes)

1. Introduce the topic by saying something like this:

Last time, we talked about the symptoms you may get if you have heat exhaustion or the very serious condition called heat stroke. Today we are going to talk about what you should do if you or your co-workers are having these symptoms.

2. Ask the crew these questions:

(Wait for their answers and then use the shaded answer boxes to add any information they missed.)

Let's say there is a worker in our crew who has signs of heat exhaustion: she is very sweaty, weak, and has a headache. What do you think you should do?

1. Notify the supervisor. She needs medical help.

2. Move the person to a cooler place to rest in the shade. Don't leave her alone.

3. Little by little, give her water.

4. Loosen her clothing.

5. Help cool the person. Fan her, put ice packs on her groin and underarms, or soak her clothing with cool water.

3. Add the following points:

Be prepared to describe the symptoms and know how to describe our location to the emergency personnel so they can find us quickly.

Don't wait because heat exhaustion can quickly become more dangerous.

Be alert to unusual behavior: if your co-workers seem confused, or are sitting by themselves or walking around aimlessly, ask them if they're okay. If they seem to be acting strangely, they may have heat stroke. Contact the supervisor.

4. For the next activity pick one of the workers to be a person who has heat exhaustion, and explain:

(Make sure the crew acts out what they would do, instead of just telling you. Add any points they miss from the shaded box below.)

Now to review how we would respond, you are going to practice what you should do if someone is having symptoms of heat exhaustion.

Let's say you are working with _(fill in name)_ and you notice he is very sweaty and confused, and he looks disoriented and can't seem to concentrate on his work. Show me what you would do.

> 1. Call the supervisor and asks for medical help.
>
> 2. Move the person to a cooler place to rest in the shade. Stay with the person.
>
> 3. Give the person water as long as he/she is not losing consciousness or vomiting.
>
> 4. Loosen the person's clothing.
>
> 5. Help cool the person. Fan the person, put ice packs on the person's groin and underarms, or soak the person's clothing with cool water.

5. To conclude, ask if anyone has questions, then close by saying:

Now we have learned how we would respond if someone developed heat exhaustion, but the best strategy is always prevention. Next time, we are going to talk about how to prevent heat exhaustion.

Training Session #3: Preventing Heat Exhaustion

(Time: 15 minutes)

1. *Introduce the topic by saying something like this:*

   While heat exhaustion is very dangerous, it is also preventable. Today we are going to review what we have learned so far and talk about what we can do to protect ourselves from heat. There are three simple words: water, rest, shade. Heat illness can be prevented: Drink water often, even if you aren't thirsty; rest in the shade to cool down; report heat symptoms early; know what to do in an emergency.

2. *Show the crew the drawing of Rogelio on page 31. Read the following story out loud:*

   Rogelio is a new member of a crew that is picking melons in the fields. On his second day, he works hard for long periods without a break. In the early afternoon his co-worker, Julio, looks over and sees that Rogelio is sweating profusely and is acting strangely. Julio asks Rogelio what's going on, and Rogelio says he has a slight headache and feels dizzy.

   Julio realizes Rogelio needs help and calls the crew leader. Together they give him water and help him sit down. Julio stays with him while the crew leader calls 911 for medical help.

   Rogelio recovers, but can't work for a few days. Later, he says he had wanted to show he could work hard, and he didn't drink much water because he didn't feel thirsty.

3. Ask the crew these questions:

(Wait for their answers and then use the shaded answer boxes to add any information they missed.)

How do you know Rogelio may be suffering from heat exhaustion?

> - He is sweating, weak, has a headache, and feels dizzy.

What went well in this case to address heat exhaustion?

> - Julio called the crew leader.
> - They gave Rogelio water.
> - They called 911.
> - They helped him sit down to rest.
> - Julio was watching out for his co-worker. He stayed with Rogelio while the crew leader made the call.

What went wrong?

> - Rogelio wasn't used to working in the heat. He should have had less intense work until he got used to working in the heat.
> - They had not made sure Rogelio got adequate breaks.
> - Rogelio hadn't drunk water. You shouldn't wait until you are thirsty to drink.
> - They didn't take Rogelio to shade.
> - Rogelio wanted to prove he could work hard — he didn't report symptoms as soon as he felt them.

So what can we learn from this – what are the important steps to prevent heat exhaustion?

> - Rogelio wasn't used to working in the heat. He should have had less intense work until he got used to working in the heat.
>
> - They had not made sure Rogelio got adequate breaks.
>
> - Rogelio hadn't drunk water. You shouldn't wait until you are thirsty to drink.
>
> - They didn't take Rogelio to shade.
>
> - Rogelio wanted to prove he could work hard – he didn't report symptoms as soon as he felt them.

4. Add the following points:

It is recommended that each person drink water often.

- It's better to drink small amounts frequently, as opposed to larger amounts less often.

- Drink even if you don't feel thirsty.

- Avoid drinks like sodas or coffee that have caffeine, or alcoholic drinks – these drinks dehydrate you and can make it more dangerous to work in the heat. Also avoid sports drinks as these contain too much sugar.

- People worry that if they drink a lot of water, they'll have to go to the bathroom more often. In fact, you'll mostly sweat it off.

- When you're not at work, still drink plenty of water to help your body recover from the workday.

- During a heat wave, it is recommended to provide more frequent breaks.

- Pair off and watch your co-worker for signs of heat exhaustion. Remind your buddy to drink water or take a break. Talk to your buddy during the work shift to make sure everything is okay. Sometimes people with heat exhaustion get disoriented and think they are okay. If you suspect a problem, keep checking on your co-worker or tell a supervisor.

- Sometimes people say they are more protected by dark-colored, heavier clothing. This will only make you hotter. Wear light-colored lightweight cotton clothing.

5. Explain to the crew:

There are also ways to prevent heat exhaustion that have to do with how the work is done. At our site we will: *(check those that apply to your site)*

☐ Schedule our work to do the more strenuous tasks during cooler times of the day.

☐ Start work earlier and end earlier.

☐ Add more scheduled breaks.

☐ Other: _____

6. Ask the crew this question:

What other suggestions do you have for what we can do on this job site to prevent heat exhaustion?

(Give the crew a few minutes to come up with suggestions. Make a plan for implementing good ideas.)

7. To conclude, ask if anyone has questions and remind workers of the following four points:

1) Drink water often; 2) Rest in the shade; 3) Report heat symptoms early; 4) Know what to do in an emergency.

Drink water often

Rest in the shade

Report heat symptoms early

Know what to do in an emergency

Daily Checklist ☑

This is a helpful guide that you may choose to use before each workday.

Drink water often

Rest in the shade

Report heat symptoms early

Know what to do in an emergency

Checklist		☑
Water	Is there plenty of fresh, cool drinking water located as close as possible to the workers?	
	Are water coolers refilled throughout the day?	
Shade	Is there shade available for breaks and if workers need to recover?	
Training	Do workers know the:	
	Common signs and symptoms of heat illness?	
	Proper precautions to prevent heat illness?	
	Importance of acclimatization?	
	Importance of drinking water frequently (even when they are not thirsty)?	
	Steps to take if someone is having symptoms?	
Emergencies	Does everyone know who to notify if there is an emergency?	
	Can workers explain their location if they need to call an ambulance?	
	Does everyone know who will provide first aid?	
Worker Reminders	Drink water often	
	Rest in shade	
	Report heat symptoms early	
	Know what to do in an emergency	

OSHA Publications

- OSHA Heat Safety Fact Sheet, Publication #3422; English

- OSHA Heat Safety Fact Sheet, Publication #3423; Spanish

- OSHA Worksite Poster, Publication #3431; English

- OSHA Worksite Poster, Publication #3432; Spanish

- OSHA Community Poster, Publication #3435; English

- OSHA Community Poster, Publication #3436; Spanish

For Use in Training

- Rogelio's Story

- Diagram #1. Preventing Heat Illness

- Diagram #2. Health Effects of Heat

WATER.
REST.
SHADE.

The work can't get done without them.

 **A HEAT SAFETY FACT SHEET**

Two types of heat illness:

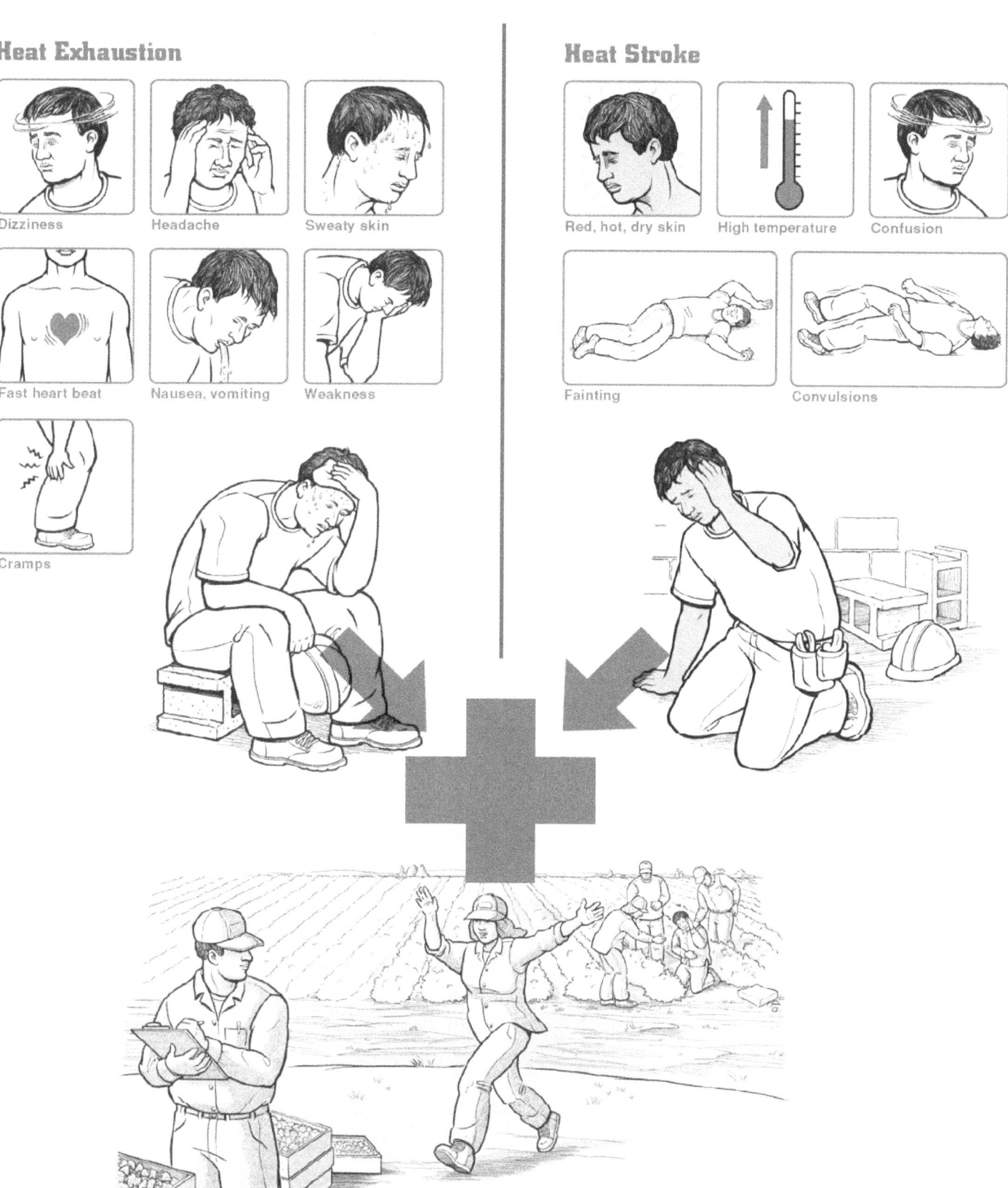

Heat Exhaustion

Dizziness

Headache

Sweaty skin

Fast heart beat

Nausea, vomiting

Weakness

Cramps

Heat Stroke

Red, hot, dry skin

High temperature

Confusion

Fainting

Convulsions

*Heat kills – **get help right away!***

Stay safe and healthy!

Drink water even if you aren't thirsty — *every 15 minutes*

Watch out for each other

Wear a hat and light-colored clothing

Know where you are working in case you need to call 911

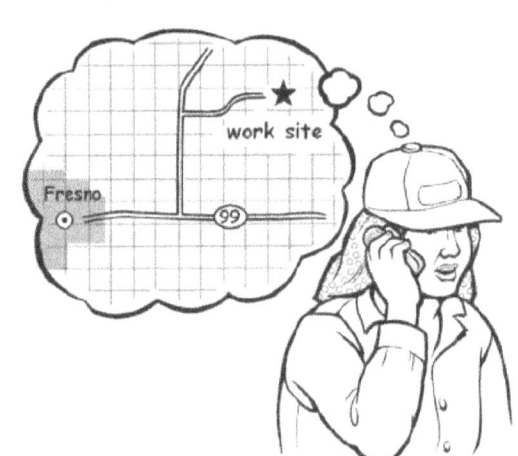

Rest in the shade

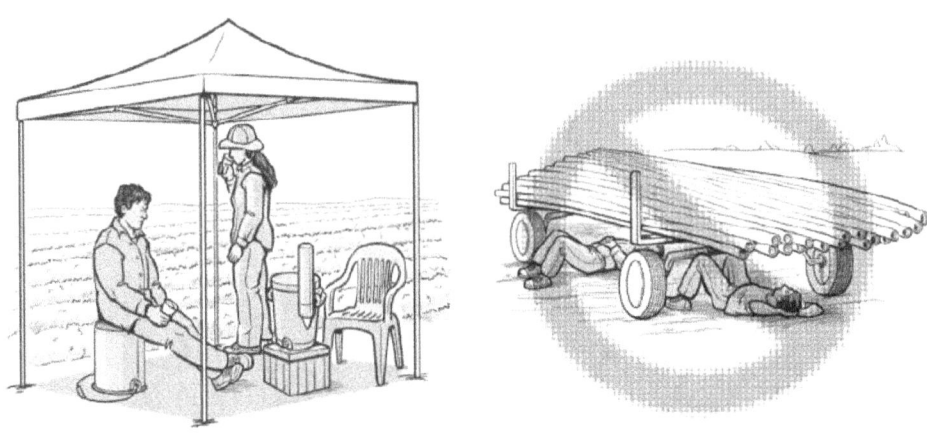

Heat illness can be prevented!

 ☑ **Water**

☑ **Shade and Rest**

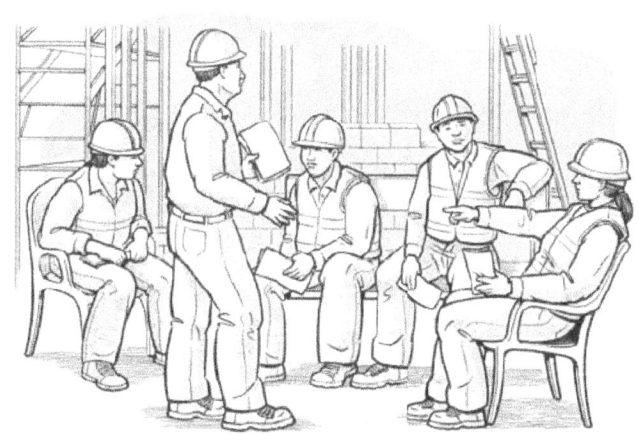

☑ **Training**

☑ **Emergency Plan**

U.S. Department of Labor
Hilda L. Solis, Secretary of Labor

Developed by
CAL/OSHA

If you have questions, call OSHA.
It's confidential. We can help!
1-800-321-OSHA (6742)
TTY 1-877-889-5627
www.osha.gov

OSHA 3422-04N 2011

AGUA.
SOMBRA.
DESCANSOS.

Sin ellos no se puede trabajar.

 **UNA HOJA INFORMATIVA SOBRE EL CALOR**

Dos tipos de enfermedades por calor:

Agotamiento

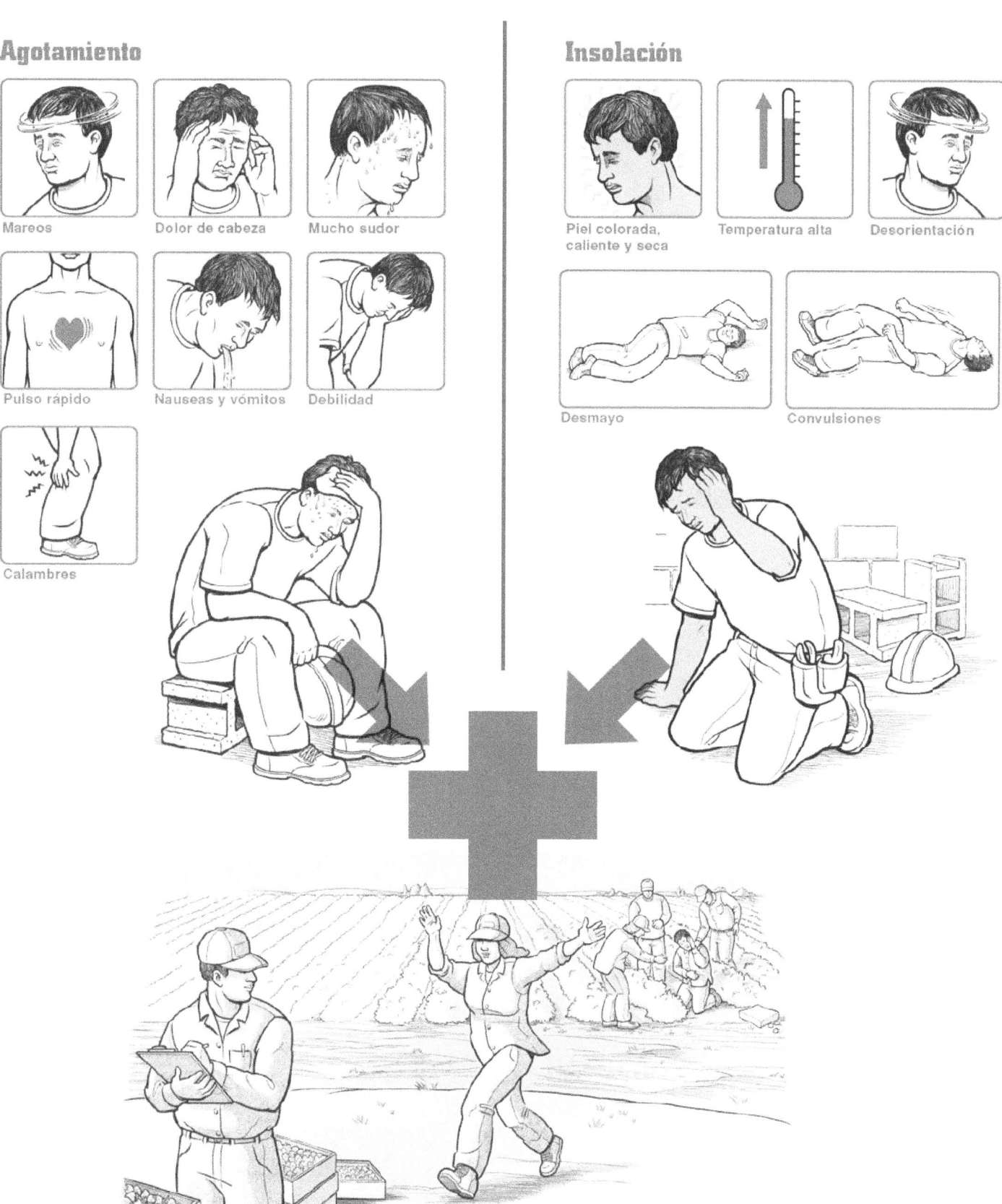

Mareos

Dolor de cabeza

Mucho sudor

Pulso rápido

Nauseas y vómitos

Debilidad

Calambres

Insolación

Piel colorada, caliente y seca

Temperatura alta

Desorientación

Desmayo

Convulsiones

El calor mata – ¡Consiga ayuda de inmediato!

¡Manténgase seguro y sano!

Tome agua aunque no tenga sed – *cada 15 minutos*

Esté pendiente de sus compañeros

Use sombrero y ropa ligera de colores claros

Sepa dónde está trabajando por si necesita llamar al 911

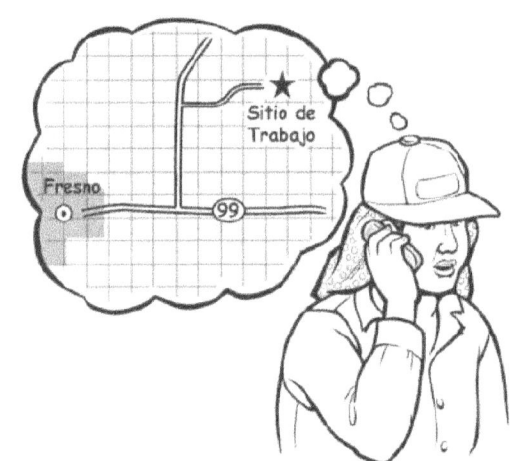

Descanse en la sombra

¡Se pueden prevenir las enfermedades por calor!

☑ **Agua**

☑ **Sombra y descansos**

☑ **Capacitación**

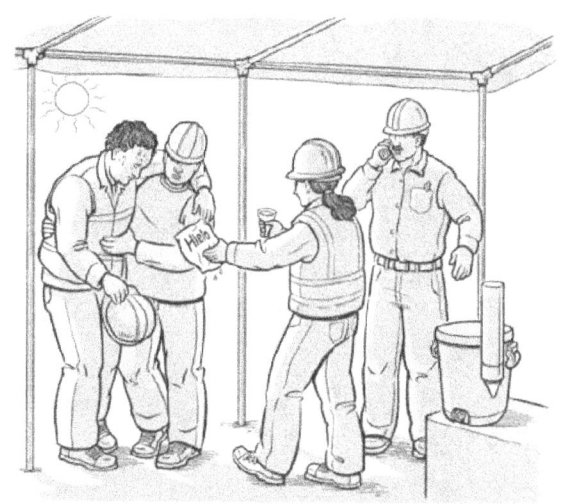

☑ **Plan de emergencia**

Departamento de Trabajo de E.E.U.U.
Hilda L. Solis, Secretaria del Departamento
del Trabajo de los Estados Unidos

CAL OSHA

Desarrollado por
CAL/OSHA

Si usted tiene preguntas, llame a OSHA.
Esta información es confidencial.
¡Nosotros podemos ayudar!
1-800-321-OSHA (6742) • TTY 1-877-889-5627 • www.osha.gov

OSHA 3423-04N 2011SP

Health effects of heat
Two types of heat illness:

Heat Exhaustion

Heat Stroke

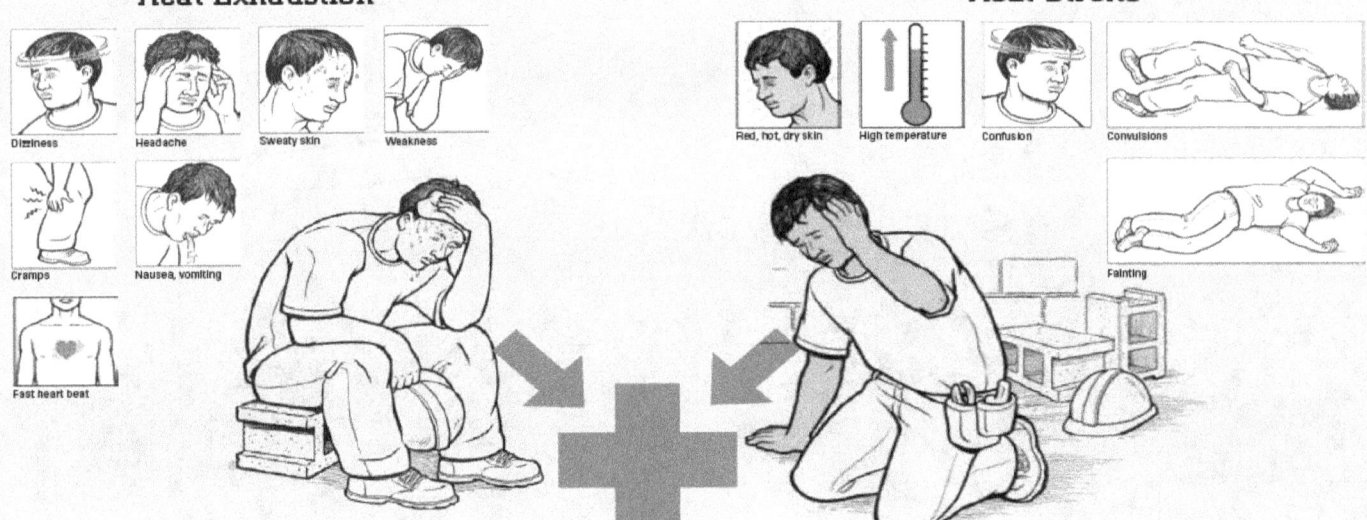

Watch out for early symptoms. You may need medical help.
People react differently — you may have just a
few of these symptoms, or most of them.

1

Stay safe and healthy!
WATER. REST. SHADE. The work can't get done without them.

Drink water even if you aren't thirsty — every 15 minutes.

Rest in the shade.

Watch out for each other.

Wear hats and light-colored clothing.

"Easy does it" on your first days of work in the heat. You need to get used to it.
Rest in the shade — at least 5 minutes as needed to cool down.

2

Be prepared for an emergency
Heat kills -- get help right away!

If someone in your crew has symptoms:

1) Tell the person who has a radio/phone and can call the supervisor – you need medical help.

2) Start providing first aid while you wait for the ambulance to arrive.

3) Move the person to cool off in the shade.

4) Little by little, give him water (as long as he is not vomiting).

5) Loosen his clothing.

6) Help cool him: fan him, put ice packs in groin and underarms, or soak his clothing with cool water.

When you call for help, you need to:

• Be prepared to describe the symptoms.

• Give specific and clear directions to your work site.

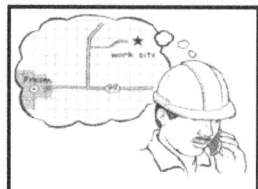

3

Heat illness can be prevented!
At our work site, we have:

Water

We are extra careful when there is a heat wave or temperature goes up. Then we may change our work hours, and we all need more water and rest.

Shade to rest and cool down

Training and emergency plan

U.S. Department of Labor
Hilda L. Solis, Secretary of Labor

CAL/OSHA
Developed by
CAL/OSHA

For more information.
1-800-321-OSHA (6742) • TTY 1-877-889-5627 • www.osha.gov

OSHA 3431-04N 2011

4

Los efectos del calor
Dos tipos de enfermedades por calor:

Agotamiento

Mareos
Dolor de cabeza
Mucho sudor
Debilidad
Calambres
Náuseas y vómitos
Pulso rápido

Insolación

Piel colorada, caliente y seca
Temperatura alta
Desorientación
Convulsiones
Desmayo

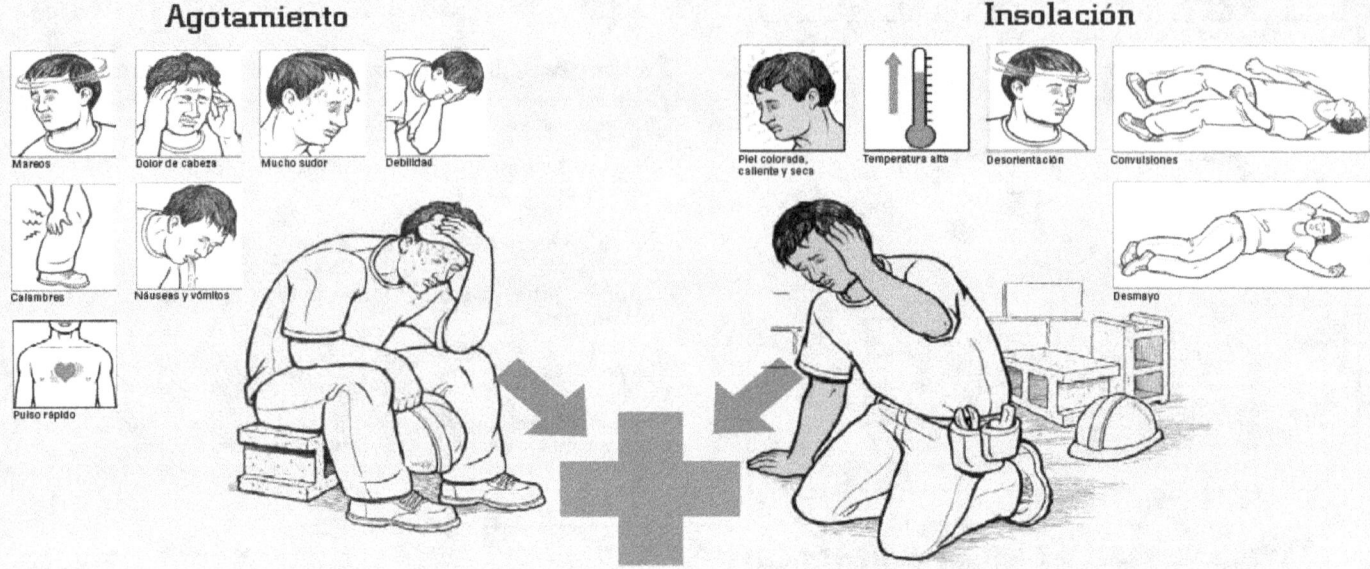

OJO con los primeros síntomas. Podrían necesitar atención médica.
Las personas reaccionan de diferentes maneras.
Podrían tener unos cuantos de estos síntomas o la mayoría de ellos.

1

¡Manténganse seguros y sanos!
AGUA. SOMBRA. DESCANSOS. *Sin ellos no se puede trabajar.*

Tomen agua aunque no tengan sed — cada 15 minutos.

Descansen en la sombra.

Estén pendientes de sus compañeros.

Usen sombrero y ropa ligera de colores claros.

No deben esforzarse demasiado los primeros días que trabajan en el calor.
Tienen que acostumbrarse. Tomen descansos en la sombra—por lo menos
5 minutos para refrescarse.

2

Estén listos para una emergencia
El calor mata – ¡Consigan ayuda de inmediato!

Si alguien en la cuadrilla tiene síntomas:

1) Avísenle a la persona en su cuadrilla que tiene un teléfono/radio para que se comunique con el supervisor – necesitan ayuda médica.

2) Empiecen a darle primeros auxilios hasta que llegue la ambulancia.

3) Muevan a la persona a la sombra para refrescarla.

4) Dénle agua, poco a poco, siempre y cuando no esté vomitando.

5) Aflójenle la ropa.

6) Ayúdenle a refrescarse. Usen un abanico, pónganle compresas de hielo en la ingle y las axilas, o empapen la ropa con agua fresca.

Cuando pidan ayuda médica, asegúrense de que:

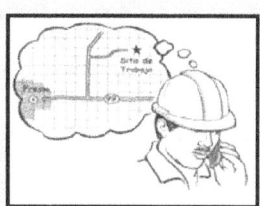

- Estén listos para describir los síntomas.
- Sepan describir su ubicación y cómo llegar a su lugar de trabajo.

3

¡Se pueden prevenir las enfermedades por calor!
En nuestro lugar de trabajo, tenemos:

Agua

Tomamos precauciones adicionales durante las olas de calor o cuando aumenta el calor. Podríamos cambiar las horas de trabajo y todos necesitamos aun más agua y descansos.

Sombra para descansar y refrescarse

Capacitación y plan de emergencia

Departamento de Trabajo de E.E.U.U.
Hilda L. Solis, Secretaria del Departamento del Trabajo de los Estados Unidos

Desarrollado por
CAL/OSHA

Para más información:
1-800-321-OSHA (6742) • TTY 1-877-889-5627 • www.osha.gov

4

OSHA 3432-04N 2011SP

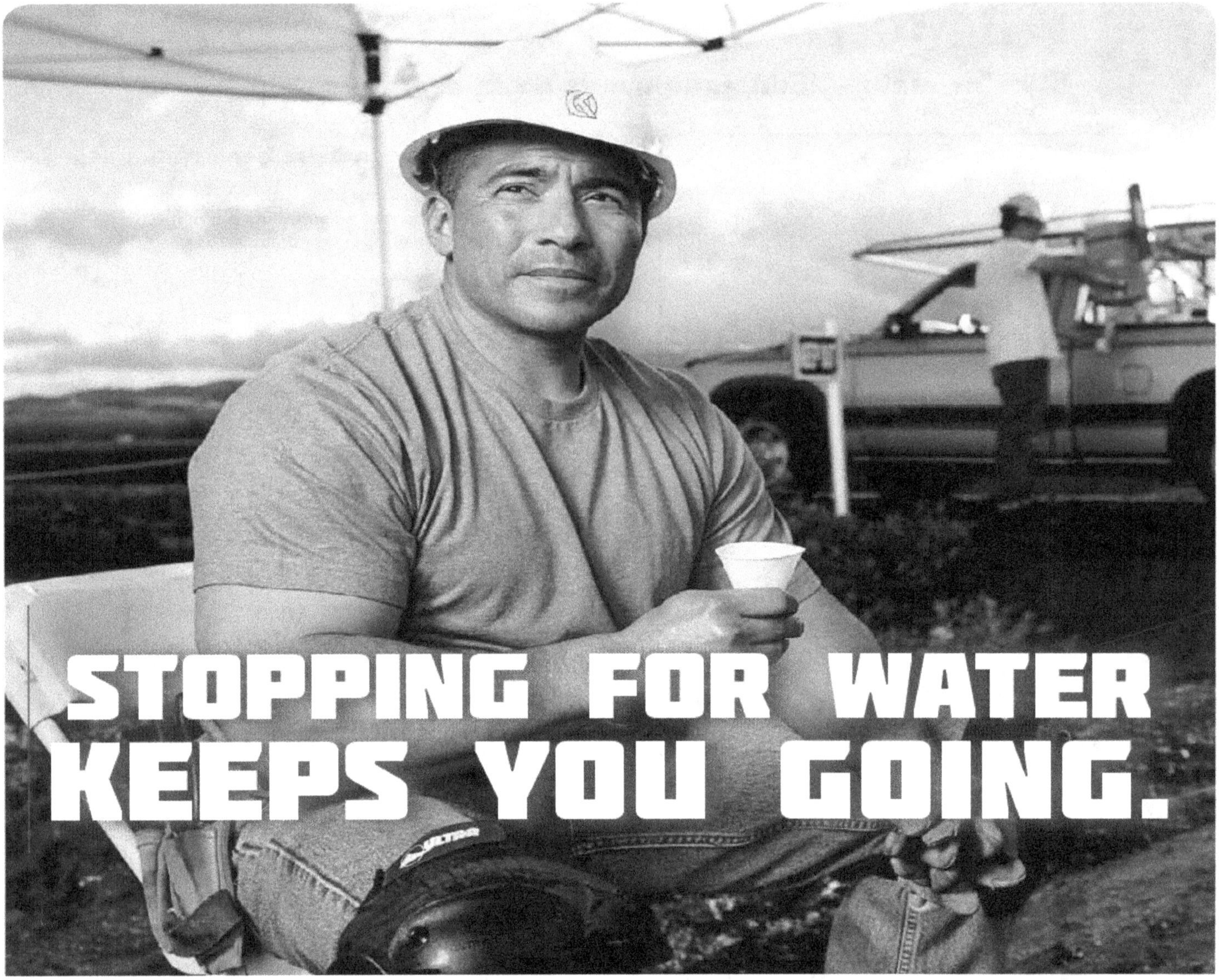

STOPPING FOR WATER KEEPS YOU GOING.

WATER.
REST.
SHADE.

1-800-321-OSHA (6742)
TTY 1-877-889-5627
www.osha.gov

The work can't get done without them.

HEAT ILLNESS CAN BE DEADLY.

Remember to:

- Drink water often, even if you aren't thirsty.
- Rest in the shade to cool down.
- Report heat symptoms early.
- Know what to do in an emergency.

Let's make heat safety part of the job. If you have questions, call OSHA. It's confidential. We can help!

OSHA 3435-04N 2011

Developed by Cal/OSHA

U.S. Department of Labor
Hilda L. Solis, Secretary of Labor

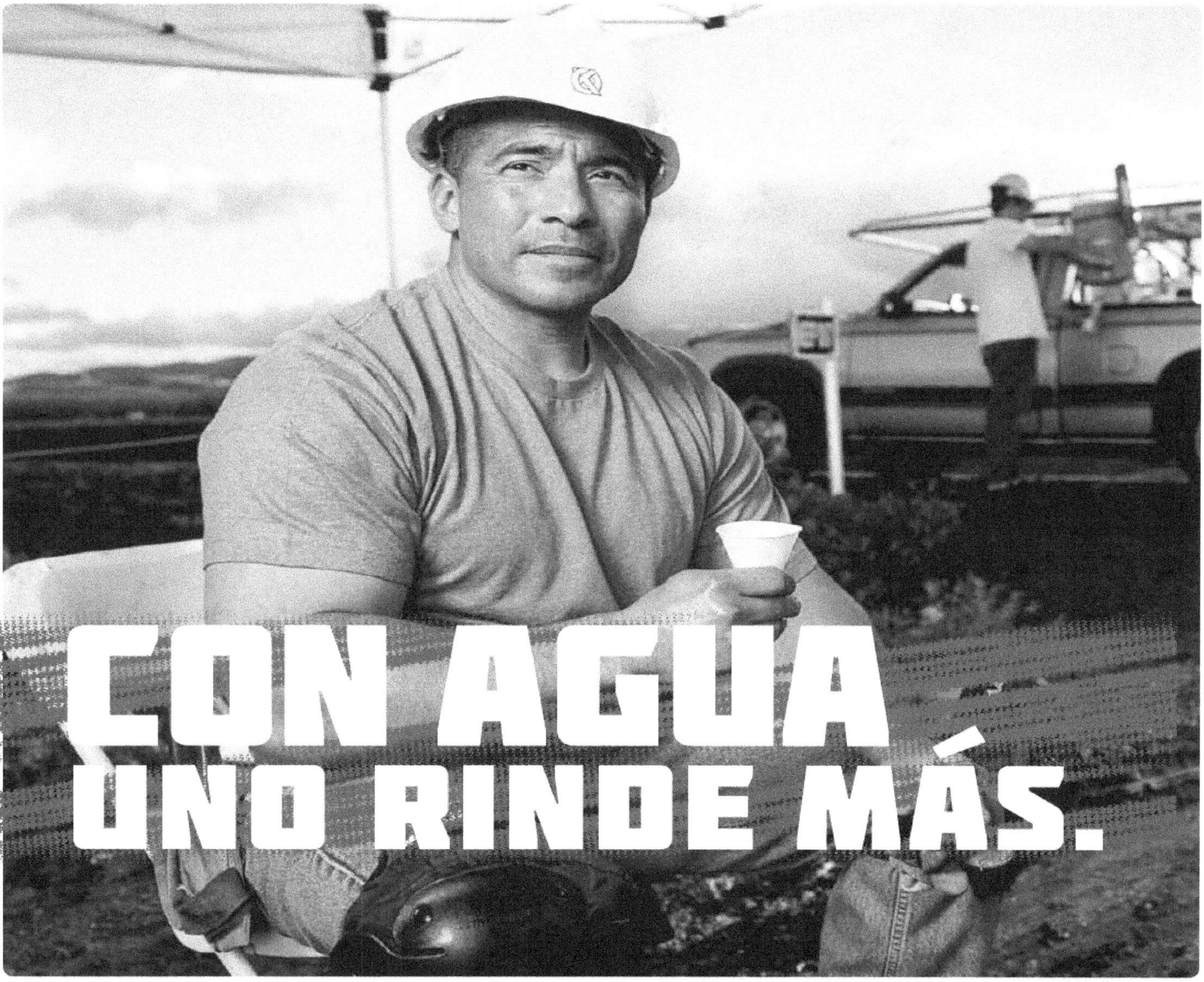

CON AGUA
UNO RINDE MÁS.

AGUA.
SOMBRA.
DESCANSOS.

1-800-321-OSHA (6742)
TTY 1-877-889-5627
www.osha.gov

Sin ellos no se puede trabajar.

EL CALOR PUEDE MATAR.

No olvide:

- Tome agua con frecuencia – aunque no tenga sed.
- Descanse en la sombra para refrescarse.
- Ojo con los primeros síntomas—repórtelos.
- Sepa qué hacer en una emergencia.

La seguridad en el calor debe ser parte del trabajo. Si usted tiene preguntas, llame a OSHA. Ésta información es confidencial. ¡Nosotros podemos ayudar!

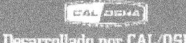

Desarrollado por CAL/OSHA

Departamento de Trabajo de E.E.U.U.
Hilda L. Solis, Secretaria del Departamento del Trabajo de los Estados Unidos

Rogelio's Story

Diagram #1. Preventing Heat Illness

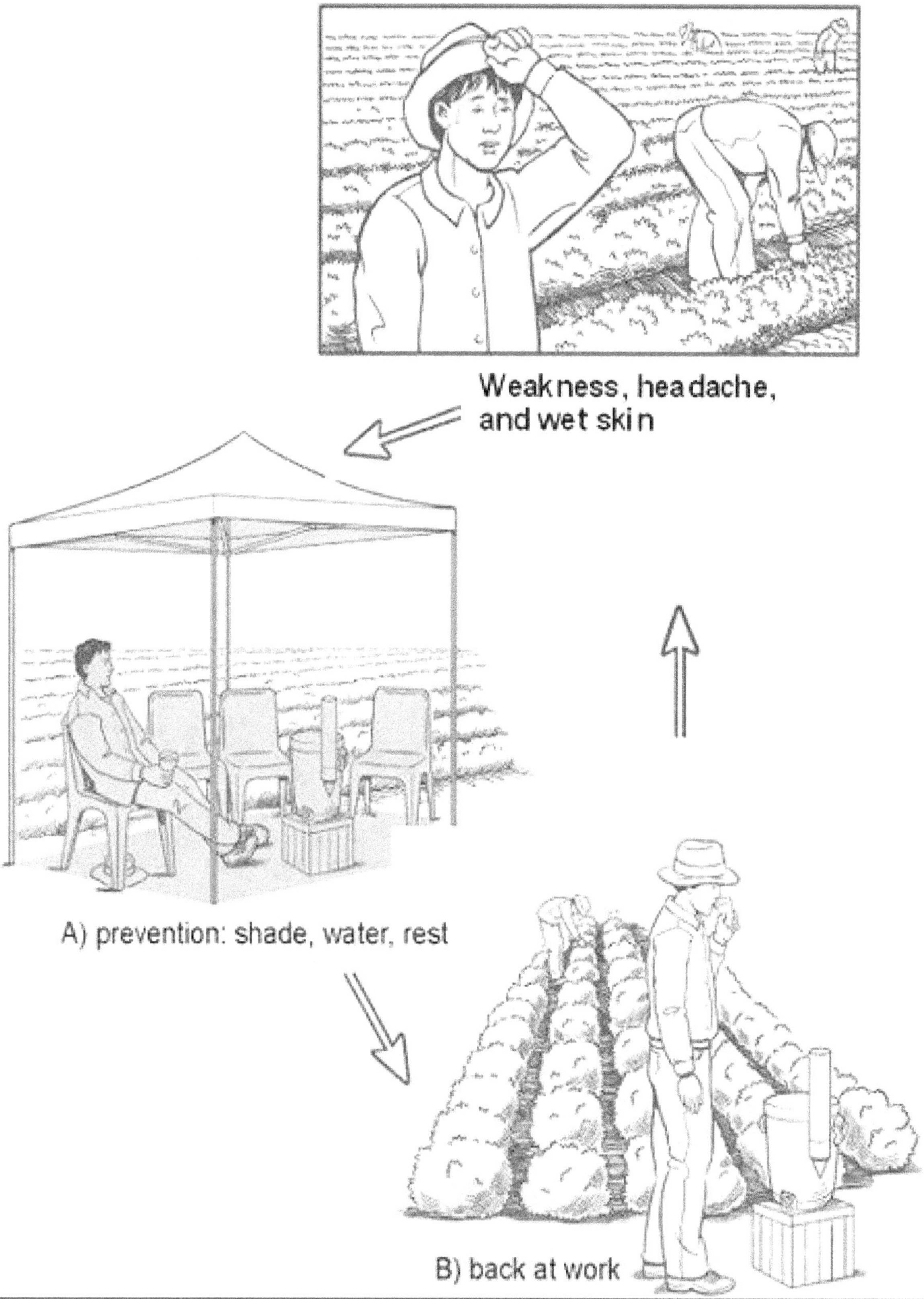

Weakness, headache, and wet skin

A) prevention: shade, water, rest

B) back at work

Diagram #2. Health Effects of Heat

Weakness, headache, and wet skin

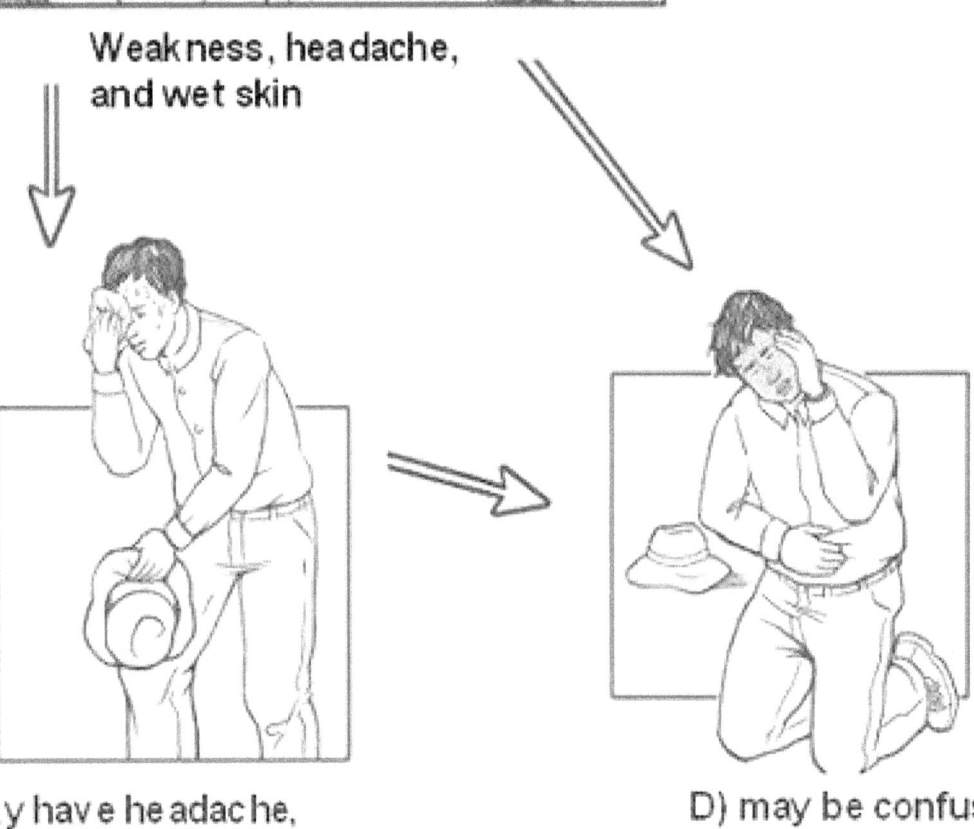

C) may have headache, dizziness, or fainting, weakness and wet skin, irritability or confusion, thirst, nausea, or vomiting

D) may be confused, unable to think clearly, pass out, collapse, or have seizures (fits), may stop sweating

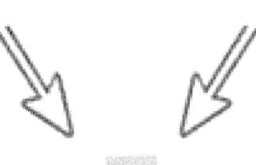

NEED MEDICAL HELP